AFTER I'M GONE

GOTHAM BOOKS
Published by Penguin Group (USA) Inc.
375 Hudson Street, New York, New York 10014, U.S.A.
Penguin Group (Canada), 90 Eglinton Avenue East, Suite 700, Toronto, Ontario M4P 2Y3, Canada (a
division of Pearson Penguin Canada Inc.); Penguin Books Ltd, 80 Strand, London WC2R 0RL, England; Penguin Ireland, 25 St Stephen's Green, Dublin 2, Ireland (a division of Penguin Books Ltd); Penguin Group (Australia), 250 Camberwell Road, Camberwell, Victoria 3124, Australia (a division of
Pearson Australia Group Pty Ltd); Penguin Books India Pvt Ltd, 11 Community Centre, Panchsheel
Park, New Delhi - 110 017, India; Penguin Group (NZ), 67 Apollo Drive, Rosedale, North Shore
0632, New Zealand (a division of Pearson New Zealand Ltd); Penguin Books (South Africa) (Pty) Ltd,
24 Sturdee Avenue, Rosebank, Johannesburg 2196, South Africa

Penguin Books Ltd, Registered Offices: 80 Strand, London WC2R 0RL, England

Published by Gotham Books, a member of Penguin Group (USA) Inc.

First printing August 2009
10 9 8 7 6 5 4 3 2 1

Copyright © 2009 by Hollan Publishing
All rights reserved

Gotham Books and the skyscraper logo are trademarks of Penguin Group (USA) Inc.

ISBN-13: 978-1-592-40457-5

Printed in the United States of America
Set in Adobe Garamond
Designed by Seth Dolinsky

While the author has made every effort to provide accurate telephone numbers and Internet addresses
at the time of publication, neither the publisher nor the author assumes any responsibility for errors, or
for changes that occur after publication. Further, the publisher does not have any control over and does
not assume any responsibility for author or third-party websites or their content.

AFTER I'M GONE

*Thoughts, Wishes,
Memories & Secrets to Share
with Those I Love*

Susan Davies, LCSW

GOTHAM BOOKS

My Name_____

I started this journal on ____/____/_____

and completed it on ____/____/_____.

How to Use This Book

After I'm Gone will provide you with specific cues
and prompts that allow you to reflect on your
past, theorize about your present, and make
wishes for your future. This book may help you
to resolve childhood issues, allowing you to live
each moment more fully. This book is a final
legacy and voice for your innermost thoughts,
feelings, desires, wishes, ideas, and plans. Filling
out this book will serve as an introspective, reflec-
tive experience, but it will also function as a way
to communicate with your loved ones after death.
Ultimately, this book is a love letter to those who
are dearest to you, and it will stand as the final
entry in the last page of the diary of your life.

CONTENTS

MY LIFE

part 1

The following entries serve as a personal record of my life, my family, and who I am. They will allow my loved ones to get to know me better after I am gone, and they will allow them to remember certain details about me that they may have forgotten. If there are any questions they wish they had asked, I hope they will be answered in the following pages.

CHILDHOOD

I was born on _____(date) at _____
Hospital in the city of _____ in the state of
_____ in the country of _____

My parents described me as

_____

_____

I would describe my childhood as: exciting / traumatic / blissful / uneventful / peaceful / fulfilling / lonely [circle any that apply].

My family moved: never / 1-3 times / 4-6 times / 6+.

The place(s) where I lived was/were

_____

_____

_____

My family was: poor / middle class / upper middle class / wealthy [circle one].

My neighborhood was

_____

_____

What I remember most about it was

_____

_____

_____

_____

_____

_____

The best word to describe my family is

_____

They taught me that

_____

_____

_____

_____

The one thing my family never understood about me was

_____

_____

_____

_____

My favorite relative was_____
because

_____

_____

_____

_____

_____

A family secret was

_____

_____

_____

_____

This secret affected me very little / somewhat / a lot
[circle one]. This secret affected me because

_____

_____

_____

_____

_____

My favorite season as a child was: fall / winter /spring / summer
[circle one] because

_____

_____

_____

_____

My favorite birthday party was when I was _____
and we

_____

_____

_____

My favorite holiday memories are

_____

_____

_____

_____

The tradition I loved most as a child was

_____

_____

_____

_____

My favorite childhood year was _____
because

_____

_____

_____

_____

The most creative thing I ever did as a child was

_____

_____

_____

_____

My favorite childhood toy was _____

Something that is made today that I wish I'd had during my childhood is

_____

_____

My favorite hobbies/activities were

_____

_____

_____

_____

My family had no / some / lots of [circle one] pets. My favorite pet was

_____

I loved to collect _____

I loved to compete in _____

I won medals for _____

My favorite sport or instrument was _____

The biggest compliment I ever got was

_____

_____

_____

_____

The person who gave it to me was_____

The most hurtful criticism I ever got was

_____

_____

_____

_____

The person who gave it to me was_____

A world event that directly affected my childhood was

_____

_____

_____

_____

I was _____ years old when it happened.

It affected me because

_____

_____

_____

_____

My role model(s) was/were

_____

_____

because

_____

_____

_____

_____

_____

I was traumatized by

_____

_____

_____

but I was able to overcome this by

_____

_____

_____

_____

The most painful part of my childhood was

_____

_____

_____

_____

_____

My earliest memory is

_____

_____

_____

_____

My funniest memory is

_____

_____

_____

A recurrent dream throughout my childhood was

_____

_____

_____

_____

My best-kept childhood secret was

_____

_____

_____

_____

I always fantasized about

_____

_____

_____

_____

What I miss most about my childhood is

_____

_____

_____

_____

The person in my childhood who most inspired me was

_____

because

_____

_____

_____

MY PARENTS

My parents got along: never / sometimes / mostly / always [circle one].

If I could describe their relationship in one word, it would be

_____

The best parts of their relationship were

_____

_____

_____

The worst parts of their relationship were

_____

_____

_____

_____

Their pet names for each other were

_____

If I ever needed advice, I would go to my father / mother [circle one].

My father / mother [circle one] always gave the harsher punishments.

My father / mother [circle one] and I were the most similar in looks.

My father / mother [circle one] and I were the most similar in personality.

My Father

My father's name is_____

and he worked as a(n)_____

_____

His educational background included:_____

_____

_____

We got along never / sometimes / mostly / always [circle one].

One word to describe my relationship with my father is

_____

My father gave me the genetic gift of

_____

_____

_____

_____

He taught me

_____

_____

_____

_____

Something I'll always remember about my father was his

_____

_____

_____

Our best times together took place when

_____

_____

_____

_____

My father was a role model to me because

_____

_____

_____

_____

Two ways in which I am similar to my father are

_____

_____

and

_____

_____

Two ways in which I am different than my father are

_____

_____

and

_____

_____

The best things about my father were

_____

_____

_____

The worst things about my father were

_____

_____

I forgive my father for

_____

_____

I would want him to forgive me for

_____

_____

_____

My father always got angry with me for

_____

_____

I am angry with my father for

_____

_____

_____

My father never gave me enough

_____

_____

My father gave me too much

_____

_____

Something I never understood about my father was

_____

_____

_____

_____

I never told my father that

_____

_____

_____

The greatest legacy my father gave me was

_____

_____

_____

_____

The legacy he gave me that I, in turn, hope I leave my children
is

_____

_____

My Mother

My mother's name is

_____

and her maiden name was

_____

My mother worked as a(n)_____

_____

_____

Her educational background included_____

_____

_____

We got along: never / sometimes / often / always [circle one].

One word to describe my relationship with my mother is

_____

My mother gave me the genetic gift of

_____

_____

She taught me

_____

_____

_____

_____

_____

Something I'll always remember about my mother was her

_____

_____

_____

My mother was a role model to me because

_____

_____

_____

_____

I felt close to my mother when

_____

_____

_____

Two ways in which I am similar to my mother are

_____

_____

and

_____

_____

Two ways in which I am different than my mother are

_____

_____

and

_____

_____

The best things about my mother were

_____

_____

The worst things about my mother were

_____

_____

_____

I forgive my mother for

_____

_____

I would want her to forgive me for

_____

_____

My mother always got angry at me for

_____

_____

I am angry with my mother for

_____

_____

My mother never gave me enough

_____

_____

My mother gave me too much

_____

_____

Something I never understood about my mother was

_____

_____

_____

_____

I never told my mother that

_____

_____

_____

The greatest legacy my mother gave me was

_____

_____

_____

_____

The legacy she gave me that I, in turn, hope to leave my children is

_____

_____

_____

_____

MY SIBLING(S)

List the names of your siblings.

_____

_____

_____

_____

_____

I would describe my relationship with my sibling(s) as:
close / formal / strained / fulfilling / traumatic / nurturing
[circle any].

_____ and I were _____ years apart, and they
were older / younger [circle one] than me.

_____ and I were _____ years apart, and they
were older / younger [circle one] than me.

_____ and I were _____ years apart, and they
were older / younger [circle one] than me.

_____ and I were _____ years apart, and they
were older / younger [circle one] than me.

_____ and I were _____ years apart, and they
were older / younger [circle one] than me.

I was similar to my sibling(s) because

_____

_____

_____

_____

_____

I was different than my sibling(s) because

_____

_____

_____

_____

_____

When we were little, our favorite games to play together were

_____

_____

_____

Sometimes our relationship was frustrating because

_____

_____

_____

_____

_____

Sometimes I envied my sibling(s) because

_____

_____

_____

_____

The best times we had were when we

_____

_____

_____

_____

Our biggest disagreements were about

_____

_____

_____

I never told my sibling(s) about

_____

_____

_____

_____

My favorite memory of my sibling(s) was

_____

_____

_____

_____

I could always count on my sibling(s) when

_____

_____

_____

_____

My sibling(s) made me laugh when

_____

_____

_____

_____

My sibling(s) made me cry when

_____

_____

_____

The ways in which my sibling(s) influenced me are

_____

_____

_____

_____

_____

_____

I always felt that my sibling(s) was/were better at

_____

_____

_____ than me.

In my mind, Mom felt

_____

_____

_____

about my sibling(s).

In my mind, Dad felt

_____

_____

_____

about my sibling(s).

I tried to help my sibling(s) when

_____

_____

_____

I want to resolve old conflicts by telling my sibling(s)

_____

_____

_____

_____

_____

_____

I feel the role that my sibling(s) played in the family was/were

_____

_____

_____

_____

_____

_____

_____

EXTENDED FAMILY TREE

(create your own digram)

BASIC MEDICAL HISTORY

My mother suffered from/died from

_____

_____

My father suffered from/died from

_____

_____

My sibling(s) suffered from/died from

_____

_____

_____

_____

Members of my immediate family have had cancer: yes / no

They are_____

_____

_____

The type of cancer was_____

_____

_____

Members of my immediate family have had heart disease:
yes/no

They were _____

_____

_____

Members of my immediate family have suffered from alcohol
or drug addiction: yes/no

They were _____

_____

Members of my immediate family have suffered from mental
illness: yes/no

They were _____

_____

I am allergic to _____

Other allergies that run in our family are

_____

_____

_____

Other hereditary illnesses that run in our family are

_____

_____

_____

My longest-living relative was _____

who was my _____, and who lived to be

_____

I try to take care of myself by

_____

_____

_____

I believe the secret to a long and healthy life is

_____

_____

_____

EDUCATION

The schools I attended were

_____

_____

_____

My grades were mostly A's / B's / C's / D's / F's [circle one].

The two things I liked most about school were

_____

_____

and

_____

_____

The thing I hated most about school was

_____

_____

I loved learning about

_____

_____

_____

I excelled at

_____

_____

_____

The subject that bored me the most was

_____

My favorite teacher was

_____

because (s)he taught me

_____

_____

My worst teacher was

_____

because (s)he was.

_____

_____

What I remember most about elementary school was

_____

_____

_____

What I remember most about middle school was

_____

_____

_____

What I remember most about high school was

_____

_____

_____

What I remember most about college was

_____

_____

_____

What I remember most about graduate school was

_____

_____

_____

The one thing school never taught me was

_____

_____

_____

_____

_____

_____

The person from whom I learned the most about life was

_____

_____

The place from which I learned the most about life was

_____

_____

FRIENDS

My best friend as a child was _____

and I'll always remember the time we

_____

_____

_____

_____

_____

_____

My oldest friend is _____

We have known each other for _____ years.

My closest friend now is _____

and I'll always remember the time we

_____

_____

_____

_____

_____

I am so grateful to my friends for

_____

_____

_____

_____

_____

_____

_____

I never told them about

_____

_____

_____

_____

_____

Without them I couldn't have

_____

_____

_____

My friends made me laugh when

_____

_____

_____

_____

They made me cry when

_____

_____

_____

_____

I can always picture my friends

_____

_____

_____

_____

_____

CAREER

I had _____ jobs in _____ years.

The longest time I spent in any one job was_____

The job I loved the most was_____

The job I loved the least was_____

I mostly worked: outdoors / in an office / at a cubicle / from home /other [circle any].

The benefits of my career have been

_____

_____

_____

_____

_____

The drawbacks of my career have been

_____

_____

_____

_____

_____

The career accomplishment I'm most proud of is

_____

_____

_____

_____

The career failure I most regret is

_____

_____

_____

_____

My chosen work has affected who I am because

_____

_____

_____

_____

The most important thing I could tell someone starting out in my chosen career is

_____

_____

_____

_____

If I hadn't been a(n)_____

I would have chosen to be a(n)_____

TRAVEL

I have traveled to

_____

_____

_____

_____

_____

Two places I wish I had traveled to are

_____

_____

If I could live in any foreign country, I would live in

_____

because

_____

_____

The best family vacation I ever went on was to

_____

because

_____

_____

The languages I speak are_____

I always wish I spoke_____

Traveling to_____

taught me so much about

_____

_____

_____

When I imagine a peaceful place, it is

_____

_____

_____

_____

My idea of paradise is

_____

_____

_____

SIGNIFICANT OTHERS

My spouse's name is _____

Our pet names for each other are

_____

We met in the year _____ when we were _____ (ages)

Our anniversary date is_____

I fell in love with my spouse's

_____

_____

_____

I feel loved by my spouse because

_____

_____

_____

_____

The most important thing my spouse taught me was

_____

_____

_____

The most important thing I told my spouse was

_____

_____

_____

One important thing I never told my spouse was

_____

_____

_____

_____

My spouse always understood me when

_____

_____

_____

I trusted my spouse because

_____

_____

_____

My spouse makes me laugh when

_____

_____

_____

My spouse makes me cry when

_____

_____

_____

My spouse was the best mate because

_____

_____

_____

My spouse was the best mother/father because

_____

_____

I would choose my spouse again because

_____

_____

_____

Our best vacation was

_____

_____

_____

The best part of our wedding was

_____

_____

_____

We had an intimate / medium-sized / large wedding.

The best part of our honeymoon was

_____

_____

_____

The most precious memory of our life together is

_____

_____

_____

_____

_____

Our most romantic experience was

_____

_____

_____

_____

My spouse surprised me when

_____

_____

_____

_____

The most meaningful gifts from my spouse were

_____

_____

_____

When I see

_____

I think of my spouse.

When I hear

_____

I think of my spouse.

I hope my spouse will remember me by

_____

_____

_____

_____

_____

My spouse and I agreed to disagree about

_____

_____

_____

We are most alike because

_____

_____

_____

_____

We are different because

_____

_____

_____

_____

I needed my spouse the most when

_____

_____

_____

My spouse was his/her best self when

_____

_____

_____

My biggest regret is that we

_____

_____

I forgive my spouse for

_____

_____

_____

_____

I would like him/her to forgive me for

_____

_____

_____

_____

My three wishes for my spouse are:

1)_____

2)_____

3)_____

CHILD(REN)

My child(ren) is/are named

_____

_____

_____

_____

We decided to name him/her this because

_____

_____

_____

As an infant, my child(ren) could be best described as

_____

_____

_____

The things that surprises me most about him/her/them is

_____

_____

_____

_____

An event in their life/lives that I am happy to have lived long enough to see was

_____

_____

_____

My child(ren) remind(s) me of myself because

_____

_____

_____

I am proud of my child(ren) because

_____

_____

_____

I feel close to my child(ren) when

_____

_____

_____

My child(ren) was/were a challenge because

_____

_____

_____

I worry about my child(ren) when

_____

_____

_____

Something I have tried to instill in my child(ren) is

_____

_____

_____

I want my child(ren) to promise me

_____

_____

_____

I want my child(ren) to understand

_____

_____

_____

When life gets difficult, always

_____

_____

_____

I hope that my child(ren) will think of me when

_____

_____

_____

My legacy to my child(ren) is

_____

_____

_____

_____

_____

_____

GRANDCHILD(REN)

My grandchild(ren) is/are named

_____

_____

_____

_____

_____

_____

The thing that surprises me most about him/her/them is

_____

_____

_____

An event in their life/lives that I am happy to have lived long
enough to see was

_____

_____

_____

My grandchild(ren) remind(s) me of myself because

_____

_____

_____

I am proud of my grandchild(ren) because

_____

_____

_____

_____

I feel close to my grandchild(ren) when

_____

_____

My grandchild(ren) was/were a challenge because

_____

_____

_____

I worry about my grandchild(ren) when

_____

_____

_____

Something I have tried to instill in my grandchild(ren) is

_____

_____

_____

I want my grandchild(ren) to promise me

_____

_____

_____

Always believe in

_____

_____

_____

I want my grandchild(ren) to understand

_____

_____

_____

When life gets difficult, always

_____

_____

_____

I hope that my grandchild(ren) will think of me when

_____

_____

_____

My legacy to my grandchild(ren) is

_____

_____

_____

_____

_____

_____

MY LEGACY

part 2

A legacy is something that is handed down from one person to the next. It can be an idea, it can be an object, or it can be a gift. In the following pages, I will discuss how I hope to be remembered, and I will share personal "gifts" with my loved ones. Some of what is written here may never have been revealed before, so it may affect my loved ones in unexpected ways. I hope they will see these thoughts, memories, and advice as insights into my true self, and find comfort in the knowledge they provide.

HOW I HOPE TO BE REMEMBERED

I would personally describe myself as: practical / imaginative / confident / timid/ extroverted / introverted / ambitious / kind/ demanding/ honest / serious/ fun-loving/ observant / independent [circle all that apply]

Two other adjectives that apply to me are

_____

and

_____

When people first meet me, they usually think I am

_____

_____

The biggest misconception about me is

_____

_____

_____

The best thing about me is

_____

_____

The worst thing about me is

_____

_____

I have always tried to be good at

_____

_____

_____

I hope you will remember me when you see

_____

_____

_____

I hope you will remember me when you hear

_____

_____

_____

Three things I want to be remembered for are

1)_____

_____

_____

2)_____

_____

_____

3)_____

_____

_____

MY VALUES AND BELIEFS

A cause I am really passionate about is

_____

_____

My biggest fear is

_____

_____

_____

because

_____

_____

_____

_____

My guiding spiritual beliefs are

_____

_____

_____

_____

I am very/somewhat/not at all religious. (circle one)

The beauty of life is manifested by

_____

_____

_____

_____

I take comfort in

_____

_____

_____

_____

_____

The world is a _____ place.

To me, God is

_____

_____

_____

_____

_____

_____

_____

I always tried to live my life by

_____

_____

_____

_____

_____

_____

MY SUBCONSCIOUS THOUGHTS AND FEELINGS

I remember my dreams: never / sometimes / often / always
[circle one].

My most memorable dream was

_____

_____

_____

_____

My worst nightmare was

_____

_____

_____

_____

The thought that most often runs through my mind is

_____

_____

_____

When I wake up in the morning, my first thought is usually

_____

_____

_____

When I go to bed at night, my last thought is usually

_____

_____

_____

A FEW OF MY FAVORITE THINGS

My favorite place to be is

_____

because

_____

_____

_____

_____

My favorite time of day is: morning / afternoon / evening / night [circle one]

During this time of day, I can usually be found

_____

_____

_____

My current favorite season is: fall / winter /spring / summer [circle one] because

_____

_____

_____

A perfect day for me would include

_____

_____

_____

_____

My favorite holiday is_____
because

_____

_____

_____

My favorite sound is_____
and it makes me feel

_____

_____

_____

My favorite poem is

_____

because

_____

_____

My favorite poet is

_____

because

_____

_____

My favorite book is_____
by the author_____
I would recommend it to_____
because

_____

_____

My favorite author is_____

because

_____

_____

_____

My favorite play is_____

because

_____

_____

_____

I have read it / seen it performed /watched it on film
[circle any].

My favorite playwright is

_____

because

_____

_____

_____

My favorite fictional character is

_____

because

_____

My favorite song is

_____

by

_____

I think

_____

should listen to this because

_____

_____

_____

_____

My favorite joke is

_____

_____

_____

_____

_____

_____

I first heard it when

_____

_____

_____

My favorite entertainer is

_____

because

_____

_____

_____

My favorite work of art is

_____

because when I look at it

_____

_____

_____

My favorite artist is

_____

because

_____

_____

_____

My favorite word is

_____

because

_____

_____

My favorite expression is

_____

_____

_____

and I usually use it when

_____

_____

_____

My favorite restaurant is _____

I usually go there with _____

and my favorite dish is _____

My favorite exercise is _____

My favorite prayer is

_____

_____

_____

_____

_____

_____

_____

_____

CHERISHED POSSESSIONS

My ten favorite personal items are:

1)_____

2)_____

3)_____

4)_____

5)_____

6)_____

7)_____

8)_____

9)_____

10)_____

I want_____to have #1 because

_____

_____

_____

I want_____to have #2 because

_____

_____

_____

I want_____to have #3 because

_____

_____

_____

I want_____to have #4 because

_____

_____

_____

_____

I want_____to have #5 because

_____

_____

_____

_____

I want_____to have #6 because

_____

_____

_____

_____

I want_____to have #7 because

_____

_____

_____

_____

I want_____to have #8 because

_____

_____

_____

_____

I want_____to have #9 because

_____

_____

_____

_____

I want_____to have #10 because

_____

_____

_____

_____

JOYS AND REGRETS

I am most grateful for

_____

_____

_____

_____

_____

_____

_____

The happiest period of my life was when

_____

_____

_____

_____

_____

The most difficult period of my life took place when

_____

_____

_____

_____

I have: few / some / many [circle one] regrets.

My biggest regret is

_____

_____

_____

_____

_____

If I had a chance to live my life all over again, I would change: nothing / a few things / everything [circle one].

What I'd do differently is

_____

_____

_____

_____

_____

Something I would never change about my life is

_____

_____

_____

_____

_____

_____

Something I'd like to change about my life is

_____

_____

_____

_____

_____

_____

If I had three wishes, they would be

1)_____

_____

2)_____

_____

3)_____

_____

LIFE LESSONS AND ADVICE

During difficult times, I remind myself that

_____

_____

_____

_____

_____

My best coping mechanism is

_____

_____

_____

The best piece of advice that was ever given to me was from

_____

who said that

_____

_____

_____

The least helpful advice ever given to me was from

_____

who said that

_____

_____

_____

My life has meaning because

_____

_____

_____

_____

I believe our time on earth is

_____

_____

_____

_____

_____

I believe the secret to life is

_____

_____

_____

_____

_____

CONFESSIONS

I feel most vulnerable when

_____

_____

_____

_____

_____

I worry a lot about

_____

_____

_____

_____

_____

I am able to relax when

_____

_____

_____

_____

_____

Something most people don't know about me is

_____

_____

_____

_____

Someone I really admire is_____
because

_____

_____

_____

_____

I never told anyone that

_____

_____

_____

_____

I've kept this a secret because

_____

_____

_____

_____

_____

I'm sharing it now because

_____

_____

_____

_____

_____

Revealing it makes me feel

_____

_____

_____

_____

_____

Something I always wanted to do but never got the chance
to was

_____

_____

_____

_____

The things I will miss most from my life are

_____

_____

_____

_____

Something I won't miss is

_____

_____

_____

_____

The hardest thing to admit here is

_____

_____

_____

_____

THOUGHTS ON DEATH

If reincarnation exists, I want to return as a

_____

If there is life after death, I believe

_____

_____

_____

_____

_____

I anticipate my next journey to be

_____

_____

_____

_____

_____

I believe my spirit will live on through

_____

_____

_____

_____

MY VISION FOR THE FUTURE

Celebrate my life by

_____

_____

_____

_____

_____

_____

The most precious gift I can leave behind is

_____

_____

_____

_____

_____

_____

I hope that in the future my spouse will

_____

_____

_____

_____

_____

_____

I hope that in the future my sibling(s) will

_____

_____

_____

_____

_____

_____

I hope that in the future my child(ren) will

_____

_____

_____

_____

_____

_____

I hope that in the future my grandchild(ren) will

_____

_____

_____

_____

_____

_____

I hope that in the future my friends will

_____

_____

_____

_____

_____

_____

_____

_____

The greatest legacy I can leave to my loved ones is

_____

_____

_____

_____

_____

_____

_____

_____

_____

_____

The greatest legacy I can leave to the world is

_____

_____

_____

_____

_____

_____

_____

_____

_____

_____

_____

_____

_____

_____

_____

_____

_____

_____

_____

_____

INDIVIDUAL MESSAGES TO MY LOVED ONES

_____

_____

_____

_____

_____

_____

_____

_____

_____

_____

_____

_____

_____

_____

_____

_____

_____

_____

_____

_____

_____

INDIVIDUAL MESSAGES TO MY LOVED ONES

FAVORITE PHOTOS OF MYSELF

FAVORITE PHOTOS OF MYSELF

FAVORITE PHOTOS OF MY LOVED ONES

FAVORITE PHOTOS OF MY LOVED ONES

MY FINAL WISHES

part 3

The following pages deal with the practical details of my death. After I'm gone, this book will stand as a testimonial for my final wishes.

The hardest part about saying good-bye is

_____

_____

_____

_____

_____

_____

_____

_____

Embalming _____yes _____no.

Autopsy _____yes _____no.

DNA sample _____yes _____no.

I want my organs/tissues to be donated _____yes _____no.

They are to go

_____

_____

My obituary should include

_____

_____

_____

_____

_____

I want to be cremated _____yes _____no.

I want my ashes to be placed

_____

_____

_____

I want my ashes to be scattered

_____

_____

_____

I want a viewing _____yes _____no.

I want to be wearing

_____

I want my body to be buried at

_____

_____

Location of plot

_____

Where the title is kept

_____

_____

I want my casket to be made of

_____

_____

I want a open casket service _____yes _____no.

I want to be wearing

_____

_____

_____

I want the mortuary to be

_____

_____

_____

I want the funeral home to be

_____

_____

_____

I want the gravestone to include

_____

_____

_____

_____

I want the design to be

_____

_____

_____

The clergyman to officiate is

_____

I want a _____religious service to be held
at

_____

I want the eulogy to be made by

_____

and to include

_____

_____

_____

_____

_____

My achievements

_____

_____

_____

_____

_____

_____

My education

_____

_____

_____

_____

Military service

_____

_____

_____

_____

Honors

_____

_____

_____

_____

Interests, hobbies, and passions

_____

_____

_____

_____

Occupation

_____

_____

_____

Volunteer work

_____

_____

_____

_____

Favorite charities and causes

_____

_____

_____

_____

The music I want played at my funeral is

_____

_____

_____

_____

_____

The psalms, hymns and prayers I want recited are

_____

_____

_____

_____

_____

_____

I want the vocalist to be

_____

_____

_____

I want the musicians to be

_____

_____

_____

I want readings and speeches to include

_____

_____

_____

_____

_____

_____

I want the flowers to be

_____

_____

_____

_____

My pallbearers are to be

_____

_____

_____

_____

I want the memorial service to include

_____

_____

_____

_____

I want the memorial displays to include

_____

_____

_____

_____

My special instructions are

_____

_____

_____

_____

The executor of my estate is

_____

My heirs are

_____

_____

_____

_____

My final wishes are

_____

_____

_____

_____

_____

My lawyer is_____

Location_____

Phone #_____

Location of important documents:

Will_____

Bank:_____

My investment broker is_____

Location_____

Phone #_____

Life insurance policy_____

Policy #_____

Birth certificate:_____

_____

Marriage certificate:_____

_____

Military discharge papers_____

_____

Social Security card/number: _____

_____

Income tax returns _____

_____

Investment documents _____

_____

Citizenship papers _____

_____

Deeds and titles to properties _____

_____

My name and place of work is

_____

_____

_____

The phone number and contact person is

_____

_____

_____